Copyright © 2022 by Marie Bethel.

All rights reserved. No part of this publication may be reproduced, distributed, or transmitted in any form or by any means, including photocopying, recording, or other electronic or mechanical methods, without the prior written permission of the publisher, except in the case of brief quotations embodied in critical reviews and certain other noncommercial uses permitted by copyright law. For permission requests, write to the publisher, addressed "Attention: Permissions Coordinator," at the address below.

Marie Bethel/Author's Tranquility Press
2706 Station Club Drive SW
Marietta, GA/30060
www.authorstranquilitypress.com

Publisher's Note: This is a work of fiction. Names, characters, places, and incidents are a product of the author's imagination. Locales and public names are sometimes used for atmospheric purposes. Any resemblance to actual people, living or dead, or to businesses, companies, events, institutions, or locales is completely coincidental.

Ordering Information:
Quantity sales. Special discounts are available on quantity purchases by corporations, associations, and others. For details, contact the "Special Sales Department" at the address above.

Back In Time/ Marie Bethel. -- 1st ed.
Paperback: 978-1-958179-51-2
Ebook: 978-1-958179-52-9

Contents

The Fascination of a Tropical Country

My Childhood

Fruits that Grow in the Caribbean and the Things We Made

Christmas time

Rule by a Thumb

The History of the Trinidad Carnival

The History of My Generations

Dreams Do Come True

About The Author

The Fascination of a Tropical Country

Trinidad and Tobago is a tropical country famous for its calypso and steel bands, Genuinely, highly fresh with its balmy beaches and its windy shores, Lavish streets with fruits of various kinds and flavors, For Mother Nature is beyond its bounds.

Hear the streams, the roaring rivers as they flow, and the singing birds in the trees, The essence tone of the valleys, followed by the sweet scent of daffodils and roses! The green meadows with grazing cows on the fields, the beautiful bunches of lilies spreading across the silent rivers. a

A windy wind that blows the windmill on the hill. Smell the sweet scent of sugarcanes planted on a suited spot. See the fishes in the sea with choice of sizes and of colors, The white corals spreading itself on the sandy beach. The misty sounds of the frogs sitting on the lily pads on the calm cool waters.

The dusty streets that lead to the villages, with mountains so high and so deep, Covered with marigolds and little weeds. Which makes this place a wonderful sight? The forest with wild animals and its growing fears.

Listen to the ocean and its beat, The roaring tide and stormy wind, coconut trees and palm trees That spread across this lucky place. With shady trees that cool off the hot and sticky days. The flat pebbles that lead to nothing else but the path of a sandy track leading to the beautiful beaches.

Smell the oysters! Smell the lobsters! Smell the crabs! Smell the shrimps! Smell the fishes! Which makes this place a promised land?

Trinidad and Tobago is magnificent at its best; it is blessed with its luck, For Mother Nature has spread her blossoms on this fruitful land.

Written by Marie Bethel.

This poetry will be posted in a children's book entitled Back in Time. It was written in 1966 but never published.

My Childhood

The unforgettable years of my childhood knowledge were of the bitter and sweet days I have endured as a child. I could never disregard the memories that I had experienced in those wondering years of the countless play activities and delightful school days. It was not always the best of intervals, but we made it the greatest experience, and it was a period that was well spent. Under a shady tree, one could be seen sitting eating mangoes or climbing fruit trees or otherwise lying in a hammock under a cool spot, just relaxing. Those were the eras where, when you wanted a snack, you obtained it for yourself by picking fruits or climbing the trees. In those ancient days, there were no chocolates bars but sometimes only hard candy balls, bubble gums, biscuits, and cakes. Everything was being mad at home—bread, ice creams, cakes, and even candies. Most of the time, we would generally find our own snacks by ascending on fruit trees and picking our own produce, such as the plumes, guavas, coconuts, bananas, figs, oranges.

The coconuts are the most valuable and essential trees and have many and various uses. The green coconuts are the greatest and have excellent nourishment. A small hole is made in order to pour out the coconut water into a container for drinking purposes or simply by holding it close to your mouth; then it is sliced open, and the jelly can be dug out with a spoon and can be eaten.

Moreover, majority of the green coconuts were left to dry on the trees. Folks then hired a skillful climber to remove the dry and green coconuts. A vast amount of coconuts were loaded up in a donkey cart to be sold to the markets and to the tourists. Most of the time, the folks left it on the tree to become dry, and eventually, it would fall off the tree. In modern times, the vendors put the coconuts to cool in a large container with a huge block of ice, prepare it, and serve it with a straw.

Folks would formulate the dry coconuts by shredding and removing the hard jelly from the shells for cooking purposes or other uses. The dry nuts would be grated to make pastries or other baked goods, such as sweet bread, sugar cake, tarts.

Folks made lard and coconut oil from the dry coconuts. The oil was used as a skin cream or mixed with a pure yellow grease to apply to our hair. It was also used for cooking and was included in these fabulous dishes, such as rice and peas and callaloo, which is a dish made with dasheen leaves or spinach with lots of okras. The lard was utilized for baking purposes.

The hard barks of the coconuts were shredded to put to several good uses, such as brooms or fibers to apply for the construction of mattresses and cushions. We also used it to scrub all the kitchen utensils, such as the pots and pans, and to clean and shine the floors. The hard inner shells were used to make musician's instruments and were called shack-shacks. It was decorated on the outside and filled with beads or shells, and this procedure was created to make a loud musical sound. People also created ashtrays, purses, brooms, mats, and other ornaments. The coconut branches were stripped and used to make brooms, decorations, mats, and bags.

During those ancient days, you had to be an excellent climber; otherwise, you'd have to hit the fruits on the tree very hard so they would fall down, or you'd have to use a very long bamboo rod. Or you could hope that the fruits you could not reach became so ripe that it would drop to the ground. Perhaps a heavy rainfall might hurl them down, and sometimes, the birds fed on the fruits and threw them down.

As a young girl, I was a real tomboy and loved to hang out with the lads. We all had penknives to attend to our daily hunting for all kind of fruits and also to cut down the sugarcanes. Sugarcane is a very essential plant, and many people worked in the sugarcane plantations to support their families. It was a very hard job, but it was a way to earn money by choice, not like during the slavery days when slaves were deported to the Caribbean from Africa and India to work on the plantations. In ancient days, the plantation owners set fire to the sugarcanes, and it was cut down and sent by the donkey carts to the factories to be manufactured to create sugar, molasses, and rum, which is an alcohol drink. In modern times, the sugarcanes are being cut by machineries and loaded up by cranes and transferred to the trucks and delivered to the factory. Molasses is an extremely thick and tasty drink, but its primary use is for cooking purposes; it's also used as a laxative. We loved sucking the juices from the cane; it tasted like natural sugar.

Fruits that Grow in the Caribbean and the Things We Made

There are so many different kinds of fruit trees that grow in the Caribbean, but here are a few fruit trees with extremely sweet produce that are mentioned in this chapter: plumes, mangoes, guavas, portigals, pomeracs, cymits, sapodillas, chenets, and the list go on. The fruits that make the most delightful nourishing drinks or ice creams are the barbadine, soursop, and the sorrels.

Some of the fruits have strange names that are mentioned in this book, but there are many other varieties of produces, and it will be a very long list. I am going to scribe a few delicious fruits, such as the guava, which is small to medium in size and is round and green. When it is ripe, it turns to yellow on the outside and pink inside and have many tiny orange seeds. Folks made jam and guava cheese; the guava cheese could be cut into slices and eaten as a snack.

The portigal is a cousin to grapefruits but small and green in color with many seeds. The pomeracs are a red fruit almost shaped like a small pear, very white inside. Cymits are a small round fruit the size of a golf ball, purple on the outside and white inside. The sapodillas are small round brown fruits and creamy inside. The chenets are small round green fruits with very hard skin. The chenets have a large pinkish slimy seed that you have to suck very carefully after removing the shells. Moreover, it is extremely sweet and very slippery and can stick into your throat. Parents always cautioned us to bite this produce into half because a few children had some problems with this fruit by choking on it. Only older children were allowed to eat it.

Some produce that can be eaten with your meals are avocados, soursops, barbadine, sorrels, etc. Soursop is a very large green fruit covered with several small dark spikes all over, and it's white inside. When it is ripe, it becomes a dark-greenish color and soft to touch. The tree does not bear many fruits, probably about ten fruits on a tree, and takes a long time to grow big; that is because of its massive size. Most of all, it is not an extremely tall tree, but one still has to climb on a ladder to pick the fruit.

It was always a costly fruit to purchase, but most people had a tree in their backyard. When it was ripe, my mother would ask my elder siblings to pick the soursop.
To process this fruit, you have to remove the skin and break off pieces at a time. And it is soft, so you squeeze it and then strain it into a container. Add water and other ingredients, such as Carnation milk, white sugar, nutmeg, some cinnamon, and vanilla essence; serve it with crushed ice. It is a very thick white and delicious drink and can create a delightful ice cream.

You can also eat pieces of the fruit because it is very sweet and tasty. Moreover, it is much more enjoyable when it is prepared as a beverage. This is more likely to be a Sunday or a special holiday drink, if the fruit is available on those exceptional days. The soursop leaves are very important and used as a sedative or tea.

When older folks or younger children were sick and could not sleep at nights, it was boiled and strained into a cup with some honey or glucose and sometimes with milk or sugar added; it was offered to them as a remedy to rectify the problem. On the other hand, folks would wash the leaves and hang it to dry on a wire rack for that purpose. Moreover, the same procedures were done for orange skins; they were washed and hung to dry and also used to make tea or for abdominal pain.

The barbadine fruit is quite a large plant that grew on a heavy vine. It resembles a cucumber but is as large as a medium-sized long watermelon.

The barbadine fruit is quite a large plant that grew on a heavy vine. It resembles a cucumber but is as large as a medium-sized long watermelon. When it is ripe, it is lime green and soft. It was a very expensive produce, and only a few people were lucky to have that tree growing in their backyard. Otherwise, folks had to purchase it in a vegetable marketplace. The inside is white, and it is prepared in the same formula as the soursop. It makes a special and very delicious drink and is served with crushes of ice; it also can make a tasty ice cream.

The sorrel is a medium-height tree with several clusters of leaves and bears a tremendous amount of produce. It has small round green seeds and is surrounded with small green petals. When it is ripe, it turns into a reddish color, and now it is ready for picking. Folks would remove the petals, rinse it, and place it in the sun to dry on a thinning sheet. After it had dried, it was placed into a large pot of water with spices and boiled until the leaves became soft; then it was ready for straining into a jar. Then sugar and vanilla essence were added. It is a red drink that resembles red wine. This tree bears its fruits around the Christmas season, and it makes a delicious beverage during the holiday season.

To make ginger beer, the skin of ginger was washed and peeled and placed on a wire rack to dry in the sun and then placed into a mortar to be pounded until it was minced. Then it was poured into a huge jar filled with water and spices and then left to fumigate for several months. When my mother was ready to make a drink, she would pour some into a container and add water and sugar. Then it would be ready to drink and was served with a block of ice in your glass. It is strong but very delicious.

The same procedure was done for mauby bark; it comes from the bark of its tree. The bark was put to boil with another ingredient called aniseeds; sugar and vanilla essence were applied. This drink is served with ice, and it is great for the hot and sticky days. It actually cools off the body temperature.

We created our own starch from arrowroot or from a produce called cassava, and our clothing were very stiff with starch, especially with the cancan that made your clothes stick out. Ironing was a very hard job, and you had to light a coal pot, putting charcoals in the base of the pot and chipping up a few pieces of wood or dry sticks, then pouring kerosene on it and lighting it. Sometimes, you had to fan it if you were in a hurry. There were three cast iron heaters to put over the coal fire; when it became heated, you had to wipe it off with a piece of rag to protect the clothing from getting dirty from the coals.

If the clothing was white, you'd have to place a piece of cotton cloth over the garment for protection from burning and soiling. First, we had to wet the clothing and then roll it in a ball and place it in a clothing basket, and it must be covered tightly in order to avoid it from becoming too dry. Moreover, we usually had a cup of water to keep on wetting the garment so it could be ironed more smoothly. We had no dry cleaners, and we did everything at home.

There were many seamstresses and tailors that were hired to make custom clothing. Even older sisters were taught how to sew, and there were no stores in the village that had ready-to-wear garments. A few stores would receive their goods from England, New Zealand, and China. They sold merchandise such as jerseys, knit clothing, hats, stockings, girdles, bags, shoes, shirts for men, handkerchiefs, and toys.

People made an outdoor slipper that was called sapat to wear while doing their daily chores. It was made from wood and was carved out to suit the size of your feet. Then a piece of used bicycle tire was applied to fit your feet, which was turned over and nailed with steel tacks.

One could hear the sound of the sapat on a dark, quiet night and know who was coming up the street. When it made loud clapping sounds, we always knew it was our neighbor Miss Ralfe. This idea of Dr. Scholl's slipper originated from the sapat, and even the shops sold them in small, medium, and large sizes for twenty-five to seventy-five cents.

We created our own starch from arrowroot or from a produce called cassava, and our clothing were very stiff with starch, especially with the cancan that made your clothes stick out. Ironing was a very hard job, and you had to light a coal pot, putting charcoals in the base of the pot and chipping up a few pieces of wood or dry sticks, then pouring kerosene on it and lighting it. Sometimes, you had to fan it if you were in a hurry. There were three cast iron heaters to put over the coal fire; when it became heated, you had to wipe it off with a piece of rag to protect the clothing from getting dirty from the coals.

We created our own starch from arrowroot or from a produce called cassava, and our clothing were very stiff with starch, especially with the cancan that made your clothes stick out. Ironing was a very hard job, and you had to light a coal pot, putting charcoals in the base of the pot and chipping up a few pieces of wood or dry sticks, then pouring kerosene on it and lighting it. Sometimes, you had to fan it if you were in a hurry. There were three cast iron heaters to put over the coal fire; when it became heated, you had to wipe it off with a piece of rag to protect the clothing from getting dirty from the coals.

If the clothing was white, you'd have to place a piece of cotton cloth over the garment for protection from burning and soiling. First, we had to wet the clothing and then roll it in a ball and place it in a clothing basket, and it must be covered tightly in order to avoid it from becoming too dry. Moreover, we usually had a cup of water to keep on wetting the garment so it could be ironed more smoothly. We had no dry cleaners, and we did everything at home.

There were many seamstresses and tailors that were hired to make custom clothing. Even older sisters were taught how to sew, and there were no stores in the village that had ready-to-wear garments. A few stores would receive their goods from England, New Zealand, and China. They sold merchandise such as jerseys, knit clothing, hats, stockings, girdles, bags, shoes, shirts for men, handkerchiefs, and toys.

People made an outdoor slipper that was called sapat to wear while doing their daily chores. It was made from wood and was carved out to suit the size of your feet. Then a piece of used bicycle tire was applied to fit your feet, which was turned over and nailed with steel tacks.

One could hear the sound of the sapat on a dark, quiet night and know who was coming up the street. When it made loud clapping sounds, we always knew it was our neighbor Miss Ralfe. This idea of Dr. Scholl's slipper originated from the sapat, and even the shops sold them in small, medium, and large sizes for twenty-five to seventy-five cents.

In those dark days, we had no electricity, so you learned to sew by hand or by a Singer sewing hand machine; a few years after, we had a Singer sewing machine with a pedal. The clothing took longer to make, but when it was finished, it was well done. We learned to sew by hand from school. That particular course was called a science class. In addition, we were educated on how to keep a house tidy, cooking, baking, sewing, and embroidery. The boys learn furniture-making, carpentry, agriculture, etc.

In those dark days, we had no electricity, so you learned to sew by hand or by a Singer sewing hand machine; a few years after, we had a Singer sewing machine with a pedal. The clothing took longer to make, but when it was finished, it was well done. We learned to sew by hand from school. That particular course was called a science class. In addition, we were educated on how to keep a house tidy, cooking, baking, sewing, and embroidery. The boys learn furniture-making, carpentry, agriculture, etc.

In science class, I baked six cupcakes to take home to show my parents, and I was sitting on the bus. Of course, the girls sat in front and the boys in the back. I was so proud that I could bake. A boy named Melbourne, who was a real brat, pulled away my pan of cupcakes from my hand and ate all of it. I cried and was very upset, and the next day, I told the teacher about his ruthless behavior. The headmaster took him to his private room and spanked him for being naughty.

Parents could not control their children because they were too old or were sick, especially boys, were escorted to the school by their parents every Monday morning to be disciplined by the headmaster, who spanked them in his office. It was that time of era when teaching children good behavior was compulsory for your parents and elders. There were no obscene languages and no fighting with other children.

If a neighbor was passing by and realized that you were doing something wrong, that individual was allowed to spank you. There was nothing you could do but to go home and cry, and you wouldn't dare tell your parents about your bad behavior because you would be disciplined again. It was the only way folks knew how to raise a well-behaved child. You ate what was put in front of you with no complaints. There is an old saying, "It takes a village to raise a child," and that is true. Every neighbor in the village raised that child, and they were respected; we were like one big happy pumpkin family.

Our dishes were enamel plates, but the glass plates or china dishes were used for special occasions. We ate with a spoon, and we did have knives and forks, but we were not allowed to use them. They were only for strangers and elders. I learned how to eat with a knife and fork when I was fifteen years old. The old folks had many things, but you wouldn't dare to touch their dishes or cutleries. The same thing was true about the living room, and you were not allowed to sit in the expensive chairs. You could only sit at the dinner table

This is a true story about two men who were godparents who came for a special lunch after the child was baptized. The table was set, and one of the men was very embarrassed that he could not eat with knife and fork. He said, "I am not hungry, and I have to go home now." But he had a few drinks before he left. The other man sat by the table, and he said, "Knife and fork is for the garden. Please give me a spoon." A neighbor was passing by and saw that the other man who had left the luncheon was at a parlor, eating and drinking. He was too ashamed that he could not eat with knife and fork.

We had no phones, and when I left Trinidad at twenty-four years old, it was the only time that I knew how to use a phone. I was actually afraid to talk on the phone. I thought someone could see me. What an embarrassing time for me! And I knew nothing about going to the bank. I was ashamed when I visited a bank and did not know how to fill out the paperwork and was taught by the teller how to do it. Even now, I do not like telephones, maybe because of the quiet world I came from. Moreover, because of business, I have to use my phone; other than that, it is in my bag or in the car.

We had a gramophone, where you could put records on, just like a jukebox, but only the bigger siblings could use it. There were good times and not-so-good times, but I still feel blessed that I was taught right from wrong.

I was able to grow up as a decent woman and married and worked hard to give my children a respectable lifestyle, teaching them to know right from wrong and to always do the right things. Education came first before anything else, and you always needed to do the best you could at all times. My father said, "If you can't do it right, then don't do it at all." I enjoyed those dark days, and it made me cherish the good and the bad times; it was the peak in the dark ancient periods.

Our clothing was very simple, and most of the time, it came from our elder siblings. Sometimes, the dresses were so long and wide that usually the skirt alone could make a complete dress for my sister and me. In those days, girls were not allowed to wear trousers but only to wear dresses and skirts, and there were three-quarter-length garments covering your knees. I never had much clothes to wear because I tore every outfit my elder sisters had given to me by climbing the fruit trees.

We had our home chores to do, and we had to respect our elders, elder sisters, neighbors, and seniors. We had to do as we were told to do; otherwise, we would receive a spanking. Parents were very strict and would not tolerate bad behaviors. It was our way of life, and our days seemed longer; parents never let you sleep in, even if it was a weekend or if school was closed. Folks believed that you should not let the sun rise on you. We were up early in the morning before 6:00 a.m. to attend church or to do our chores before going to school.

We were in bed early and rose up early because there was no electricity in those days; there were only lanterns, oil lamps, candles, flashlight, and flambos. A flambo was a makeshift light. A bottle was filled with kerosene, and a heavy piece of fabric was twisted and lighted as a lamp. People did everything during the day and went to bed earlier, except when it was moonlight. The surrounding areas were very bright from the moon. We liked looking at the stars, and most of the time, we were lucky to observe a star falling from the sky. It was such a beautiful sight to view the half of the moon with a star; the star was sitting in the half-moon. It was the most wonderful thing to see. We would try not to behave naughtily because we believed that God was watching us.

The sugarcane fields were a great hiding place to get away because it was a very difficult place to find someone sheltering in the plantation. But it was also dangerous because of snakes and scorpions, and not to forget the blades of the sugarcane leaves, which were very sharp; you could receive terrible scratches or lacerations on your arms or legs.

Moreover, its cluster of long green shady leaves made it a terrific out-of-sight place, especially if a parent was angry of a child's behavior. As time lapsed, it gave the folks time to cool down, and they might spank you another time.

I am the second youngest in the family of ten children and my elder sister, who was married—eleven in all. I was always hungry and believed that I was given very small portion of food, and my daily activities had made me more famished.

One of my chores was to feed the dogs. Their names were Stalin, Ginger, and Blackie. Stalin was a brown dog, Ginger was a spotted dog with white and black spots, and Blackie was an extremely black dog. My two other siblings and myself took turns to feed the dogs. When it was my turn to feed the animals, I ate their food and fed them at the same time; if it was a good meal, they would receive less. The dogs did not have special food; they ate what was left off the table. Sometimes, my elder sisters or mother would boil extra rice for them and mix it in a large bowl with leftover peas or gravy.

As long as there were red beans (kidney beans) and pigeon peas, I would eat most of their food. I also ate a lot of fig skins and stole bread from the kitchen and poured Nestlé condensed milk in it. Boy, was I greedy!

When I was seven years old, I spent most of my spare time "teaching" either the house post or some lined-up empty bottles as though they were my students. I placed a blackboard in front of them and pretended I was a teacher, writing and drawing on every house post. Neighbors and family children never liked to visit our home because I would have them as my pupils and teach them to read and write.

Everyone thought that when I grew up, I would become a teacher or a professor because I was a clever child and loved to read and write. At seven years old, I could read any type of book. In fact, I went to school at two years old; my older sister told me that my mother said that since I could talk, I could attend school with my older sister. And I was in kindergarten class, sitting with my bottle of milk.

I did learn; I knew the tables at two years old and sang it like a song: 1:2 is 2, 2 into 2 is 1. I knew all the rhymes, and by seven years old, I knew all the tables from one to twelve. I was very intelligent and played mostly with educational games. I would play a game with the neighbors' children or pretend to be a shopkeeper and sell goods to my playmates and siblings.

My mother had a big canteen; I would take the empty cigarette cartons from my mother's parlor and made books. The sailors came abroad to export sugar at the Goodridge Bay Port. She sold food and beverages for the sailors and men that worked there. One of my elder sisters, when she was younger, was afraid of the white sailors that came to my mother's canteen because of the color of their eyes, maybe green or blue; and they knew she was afraid of them. Probably one or more sailors would open their eyes really big to scare her, and she would run away to the kitchen's cafeteria and hide herself.

My mother was like a computer or calculator, and there were no such machines in those dark days. She would serve numerous workers, and while they were eating, she would add up their bills with no errors. I admired how my mother calculated the men's bills; they paid biweekly. It was at least twelve inches long or more, and she made no mistakes adding their debts. Among the workers who paid daily, she knew exactly who took what and how much. She never stood up or wrote anything but just took the order and served them. She would hand them their bill to pay after they finished eating their lunch or dinner.

I understand that my mother left school in third standard, which is equal to grade 8. She was smart and very accurate with her customers' accounts; she would have been a great accountant.

I understand that my mother left school in third standard, which is equal to grade 8. She was smart and very accurate with her customers' accounts; she would have been a great accountant.

My nicknames were Curly Hair and Black-Eyed Peas. I guess my eyes used to look very dark, but they became quite brown as I got older. I liked going to the canteen with my mother or elder sisters.

I collected all the empty cigarette boxes and empty containers, such as Milo cans, Nestlé evaporated milk, Carnation, Fry's Cocoa cans, and the list went on. I took them home, and I would make a "shop." I would bake mud cakes and pretend I was selling them to my siblings and our neighbors' children.

At twenty-seven years old, I returned to my country, which is Trinidad and Tobago, for a holiday; and I noticed my writing as a child displayed under the steps on a large house pillar. I drew a cat above the writing "CAT." I was seven years old when it was written.

I spent some of my time at the sugarcane field, cutting down the sugarcane and peeling it with my teeth or using my penknife and chewing and slurping that sweet and delicious cane juice. My father was a foreman at the sugarcane factory, and occasionally, he brought home a few bottles of molasses. I loved to drink the molasses because it was very tasty. The only way folks knew how to raise a well-behaved child. You ate what was put in front of you with no complaints. There is an old saying, "It takes a village to raise a child," and that is true. Every neighbor in the village raised that child, and they were respected; we were like one big happy pumpkin family.

Our dishes were enamel plates, but the glass plates or china dishes were used for special occasions. We ate with a spoon, and we did have knives and forks, but we were not allowed to use them. They were only for strangers and elders. I learned how to eat with a knife and fork when I was fifteen years old. The old folks had many things, but you wouldn't dare to touch their dishes or cutleries.

The same thing was true about the living room, and you were not allowed to sit in the expensive chairs. You could only sit at the dinner table in the kitchen. We had two large benches to sit on and a long table, as you will notice in an illustration of a Christmas dinner with all my brothers and sisters and parents.

Christmas Time

The only time we had new clothing to wear at home was at Christmas and New Year. During the holidays, we never received a spanking and were given toys. Otherwise, we made our own toys; my sister and I would make fabric dolls and wooden dolls. My brothers would make scooters and cut off a broomstick to make a handle and put two pieces of board together—one standing upright and the other flat down. They nailed it and then applied two medium-sized ball bearing wheels and attached them to the bottom of the board, one in the front and the other in the back of the scooter. We sometimes used an old bicycle wheel and rolled it around the yard, padding it with a piece of stick. The boys also would make a hole in the ground and pitch their marbles into the hole; whosoever got their marble in the hole first won.

Sometimes, they would fly their kites in the sky or spin a top, as shown in one of the illustrations. Our chores were to bring water from the main government pipe to fill the kitchen barrels, feed the dogs, sweep the yard, rake out the weeds from the flower and vegetable gardens, and also water the plants. The area must be kept extremely clean from weeds and grass at all times. Moreover, I loved to see the beautiful colored butterflies that flew or sat upon the roses and other flowers. Our yard looked so delightful with the fence garnished with the red hibiscus flowers surrounding the plot. It was swept daily to keep away the weeds, and if you dropped a pin, you could find it.

It was important to make sure that the surrounding area was always kept clean to prevent snakes, lizards, frogs, and other insects from occupying the environment. Occasionally, we would find a snake because the neighbor next to us would not clean his backyard.

We had to bring water every night and fill two large barrels, and we had two huge oil drums outside set up with a spout from the rooftop of the house. When it rained heavily, the water drained from the spout into the barrels, and this was quite helpful. We used this water for bathing and to do the laundry. We loved it when it was moonlight and especially on the weekends, because we could play and stay up late.

My father would boil corns, because we had a big cornfield at the back of the house. It was a lovely time, and we ate a lot of corns while my elder sister Uline told all kinds of stories. I remember one day my smaller siblings and I had stolen the neighbor's corns, and the neighbor told our mother she saw us do it. I don't know why we did it, because we had our own cornfields. My mother took a leather belt and beat us; I was afraid of spanking and usually would run away and hide myself in the sugarcane plantations. My mother could only catch me in my bed at nights, because I hid myself in the sugarcane plantation. I remember that day I could not run away. My sister and brother had already received their spanking for stealing the neighbor's corn, and now, it was my turn.

I put out my hands and prayed, "The Lord is my shepherd. I shall not want."

My mother said, "You shalt not want," and I received a spanking.

We loved it when it was raining. Sometimes, we were naked, but most of the time, we had our underwear on. We jumped up and down in the rain. What a great moment!

And on Sundays, sometimes the neighbors' children would come over, and we would play "Ring a Ring o' Roses," or "There is a Brown Girl in the Ring. We just had such a wonderful time under the moonlight. We looked at the falling stars and made a wish; the stars were shining so brightly. Looking at the stars, we believed that there was a God, and He was watching over us. Moreover, we were happy and contented.
There were no televisions, just a battery radio. The only time we heard live music was when our neighbors and family friends came over to our house at Christmastime and played their guitars. Moreover, my aunt and her husband celebrated the festival with us, and he played his guitar. I remembered the carolers walking around the neighborhood and holding candlesticks and singing Christmas carols. My mother or sisters would give them some money and thank them for their lovely songs.

What a wonderful time as a child—no spanking, no chores, and lots to eat and drink. My mother or father said, "I will put that licking on a shelf. After the holidays, you will get a spanking."

It was the best time of my life. There were so many different types of food and beverages, and it was the only time we could have a soda. Otherwise, my elder sisters had to pick the grapefruits or oranges to make a medium plastic bucket of fruit juice and place a huge block of ice into the plastic bucket. We had no refrigerator, so we depended on the truck, which was assigned only on a Sunday and selling ice in the village and also at Christmas Eve, New Year's Eve, and Easter.

I loved Christmas when I was a child; you could hear the carolers singing in the village, the radio playing only Christmas songs, and the neighbors all cleaning and painting. Most people, including my family, bought new curtains, but a lot of folks bought new furniture and fences for their homes. Moreover, the scent of freshly baked bread, cakes, and ham smelled through the neighborhood.

Our yard was spotless; if a needle was dropped in the yard, you could find it. Neighbors and friends cared for one another and wished one another a happy Christmas. The church bells rang, and the people went to church with their families.

All the stores and shops were closed, and it was only the public places that were open, such as hospitals, police stations, and fire stations. They were accessible. But everyone was at home with their families. What a wonderful time of giving and receiving, and everyone was very happy.

It was a time of helping one another and forgiving.In those days, men, women, and children wore hats on their heads; no one attended churches bareheaded. Mostly everyone went to church on a Sunday; it was a special day, and my mother or elder sisters would make a great breakfast or cook an extravagant meal. Morning breakfast was salted fish with eggs and fresh home-baked bread and sometimes a slice of ham with eggs. But the menu for lunch was fabulous, such as peas and rice, callaloo and crabs, sweet potatoes, macaroni cheese pie, salad, meat, and juice.

During the week, we drank water, and it was not cold, but we were used to it. On Sunday, a man with a van passed around, selling ice. Everyone in the neighborhood bought ice. My mother or elder sisters would make ice cream and coconut sweetbread or pound cake. I loved Sundays with all the goodies, but during the week and Saturday, we had to obtain our own snack. It was good to know how to climb a tree and get some fruits. Otherwise, you might have to pick up the ones off the ground, and sometimes, those miserable birds had taken a bite out of the fruit.

During the moonlight, we sat down and took the shell off the green peas to prepare for the next day's meal. My sisters used to pass their time by making doilies from the empty cotton flour sacks, and they made all kinds of things, such as pillowcases, tablecloths, and even skirts for themselves. Sometimes they would dye these and put embellishments on their clothing. Sometimes, they would take a raw potato and carve a flower on it and dip it in paint and make the most wonderful border on a skirt or dress. On other occasions, they would make embroidery at the bottom of the outfits by making lovely flowers around the garment. They made so many skirts, bags, and other household items out of the cotton flour bags that the neighbor's children teased them by saying, "They are eating the flour and living in the bag." They did not pay any attention to the children and continued about their business. We had to be in church every Sunday, and this was the Lord's day. Moreover, we had to attend Bible classes every Sunday evening in order to be confirmed in the Anglican church.

Rule by Thumb

I grew up in a time where you have to be thankful for whatever your parents put before you to eat. Anything they could find to make a meal, you ate it and not complain; and if your parents said "Jump!" you said "How high?"

My father used to be a principal before he became an engineer; he was so strict, and he whacked my second eldest brother because he wanted to be a mechanic. My brother ran away and learned the trade. My father said, "No grease monkey in this house." He must find a better trade, such as a turner or machinist. One day, my father told my mother that my brother must not have any food until he obeyed. My mother had to hide and give my brother his meal. He didn't finish school but ran away from his classes to learn to be a mechanic. The owner used to pay him twenty-five cents a week.

He was very gifted and made many cars and trucks out of wood and thinning, and also, he utilized the empty barrels of the sewing threads for wheels. I was the youngest and drove a car my brother made, and all the neighbors came out to see this car. I pedaled the car down the road. He was brilliant and took the empty Carnation milk cans and created a bonnet and fenders for the minivehicles. He made a beautiful red truck; you would think he bought it. That was how excellent he was in making vehicles.

My brother became a first-class mechanic, opened a mechanic shop, and taught all the boys in the villages who were interested in becoming a mechanic. Some of the young men opened their own repairs shops and even worked in the police force as a mechanic. He was known as the greatest mechanic in the village, and his son continued his legacy. God had given him that trade because he could not read or write but could count very well. When he attended school, he failed every subject with a zero mark. But he got an A for handicrafts; he received four hundred points for his cars and trucks.

His vehicles were left for demonstration in the school showcase for many years.

His problem began when he was a year old; he fell off our concrete step and hit his head. I understand that some gray substances came out of his head; he had a very bad accident, and it left him that he just could not study. Today, he has many vehicles on the road and sometimes still work in the mechanic shop. He loves taking old cars and recycling them. He is a millionaire, and if my father could have seen how important that trade is, he would have been sorry how he did not support his son or encourage him. In those days, there were only five cars in the village, and my father had owned one, which he called Alice; otherwise, everyone rode their bicycles.

My father died when I was twelve years old from a GI bleed, but rumors were, he was poisoned by a friend for his position as a foreman at the sugarcane factory. I missed him terribly because I was much closer to him than my mother; anything I needed, I preferred to ask him. But I still thank them for taking care of me and forgive them because that was all they knew. This whacking cameand all the neighbors came out to see this car. I pedaled the car down the road. He was brilliant and took the empty Carnation milk cans and created a bonnet and fenders for the mini vehicles. He made a beautiful red truck; you would think he bought it. That was how excellent he was in making vehicles.

from generations of the slavery days; when you disobeyed or didn't do as the master asked, you got a beating or a punishment. Our parents, other folks, and the generations before grew up that way. They carried the same procedures to their children because they did not know any better. It was the only way to control their children.

In those ancient times, there were no communication devices, such as phones; if you got sick or died, neighbors would ride their bicycles for many miles to deliver that message. As time passed by and shopkeepers owned vans and trucks, if someone died, a merchant drove his vehicle around the villages and would speak on a loudspeaker and inform everyone a neighbor had died. During the earlier days, it was word of mouth; people would ride their bicycles to inform others. The whole village came to support the family. It was always a village thing; everyone cared for one another. Everyone looked after one another's houses; no stranger could hang around the village.

I will never forget the wonderful sight of the wild marigolds, daffodils, and roses growing in the pastures; the cows grazing on the fields; and most of all, the scent of fresh air, which caused one to spend more time in the meadows. Moreover, the lovely view of a small pond in the backyard next to the plantation was greatly appreciated, surrounded with delightful lilies growing wild and the frogs sitting on the lily pads.

I liked walking through the prairies early in the morning, looking at the cows grazing, and also at a certain time, at six o'clock in the a, when those little blue flowers closed their leaves as though they were sleeping. Early in the morning, I passed by and all the little flowers were all awake and the grass was wet.

Now, in modern times, their comments are about climate change. In my childhood days, the people called it the dewdrops from heaven, which watered all the grasses, plants, and lilies that grew wild on the meadows. What a beautiful sight to see early in the morning. Our yard smelled and looked so great with the many red hibiscus flowers hanging over the fence.

My elder sister's lovely roses and daffodils were an eye-catcher for the butterflies and the bees. There were many different types of flowers in the garden, and there was the sweet scent of roses, marigolds, carnations, and daffodils and, most of all, that lovely fresh air. What a lovely scene to be with the yellow marigolds spread around the garden. We had a wonderful garden, and my sister, brother, and I had to take care of the weeds and water the garden. The rain was another playtime, and most children today will never know or experience what it is like to spend time in the rain, naked, enjoying every drop of rainfall, except for the children that are living in third world countries.

We made our own games and spent our time looking at the birds, climbing trees, and sometimes doing our chores. My favorite games were hop-scotch and "There is a Brown Girl in the Ring." "Show Me Your Motion" means you have to dance or do something stupid. We attended school in uniforms, wearing dark-blue pleated uniforms with a white short-sleeved blouse, navy-blue or red ribbon in our hair, and black or white shoes. The boys wore short khaki pants with a blue shirt with short sleeves and black/brown shoes. People made most of their foodstuff, such as jam, cakes, other treats, and bread.

We had no tea bags. We measured the amount of green tea (Red Rose Tea), put it in a pot, boiled it, strained it, and then added sugar and milk; the same procedure is done for Fry's Cocoa, ground coffee, and herb tea. Our parents would tell us to go to the pasture and pick some tea. They would wash and boil it, and it made a great-tasting tea. It was always paired with brown sugar; white sugar was only used for making cakes and pastries. We had no refrigerator, so we used an icebox; it looked like a fridge, but it was a block of ice wrapped tightly in burlap bags to keep things cold, especially for people who were selling meat that was freshly used and also beverages.

We put homemade ice-cream into a wooden pail ice-cream maker; the ice was packed around the pail, which had lots of salt on it. And moreover, a piece of burlap bag covered the ice; this process kept the ice from melting, and the salt kept it hard. We turned the handle until it became very difficult to turn, and at this point, we knew that the ice cream was ready for serving. I liked homemade ice cream; it was a very precious Sunday snack served with a slice of coconut sweetbread or pound cake.

The illustrations that I have drawn are designed to show how we made life simple. Boys and girls made most of their own toys or just spent their time playing games to help them with their daily living. The children created their own toys because their parents could not afford to purchase toys. We will receive real dolls, and the boys receive cars or trucks only on Christmas. Otherwise, we made wooden and cloth dolls, and the boys would make their own cars and trucks.

It was an excellent way to recycle clothing, and nothing was being thrown out. We wore our elder siblings' clothing and wore the new clothing for church or Sunday school. In today's world, we throw out everything as it gets old, or dresses that cannot fit us anymore are sent to thrift stores. No one takes the time to remodel their used clothing so that the smaller siblings can wear them; some are tossed into the garbage can or simply sent to a used store. Processing for reuse is a good thing for the environment, and now in modern times, we are learning to recycle everything, just like in the ancient days.

Those were the days when people made everything—baking bread, sewing their own clothing, and not forgetting planting their own fruits and vegetables. People raised their cows and goats to get milk and their chickens, pigs, turkey, ducks, and whatever they needed for meat. I remembered my brothers and his friends went hunting for birds, and they shot the birds with a slingshot. They dug a hole and made a fire, put the bird on an open milk tin can, and cooked it.

The oven displayed in the illustration in this book was made from cow dung and mud. It was mixed together with water and actually mixed well and pasted on a wood-and-wire construction. This oven was quite massive and stooad on a wooden stand. It was being used by all the surrounding neighbors, who brought their bread and cakes to bake it. We never did use the oven because my father, being an engineer, had invented his own oven, and he also made ovens for his friends and neighbors, which was more efficient and quite easy to use. It was built in such a way that it had shelves, and the bottom of the oven had a hole in the middle in which a coal pot was placed into it. The coal pot had coals that were lighted, and that heated the oven. It was quite unique. He made bread pans, and it baked very well.

Half of the village that did not have an oven used to bring their doughs and cakes and placed them in this massive dirt oven. There were no shelves in this oven, but flooring. A neighbor called Ms. Ralfie, who owned it, used to put a huge set of fire sticks in the oven and closed it. It was left for two hours, and when the wood finished burning, she then took pieces of bushes and swept out the oven. Then, she would place the bread or cakes to bake, and in about half an hour, it was ready to come out. What a lovely and well-cooked brown bread.

This oven was usually used during the holidays when every neighbor wanted freshly baked bread, and they would take turns to do their baking. Christmastime was the busiest. And this oven remained heated all night, yet in the morning, it was still warm. As a child, I enjoyed that time of the year. My siblings and the neighbors' children played in the yard, and we enjoyed the moonlight. If there was no moonlight, the neighbors lighted a flambo. A flambo is a bottle that is filled with some kerosene and a piece of heavy rag; it would stay lighted for a long time. Or they might have lanterns. Sometimes, we received from the adults hot bread with New Zealand butter. It was very tasty and enjoyable, and I will always cherish those marvelous days.

We played games such as holding hands and going around as fast as we could. That game was called "Ring a Ring o' Roses." I had also liked singing, "There is a brown girl in the ring tra-la-la-la" and "Show Me Your Motion," which means you are in the center of the ring, dancing or doing something funny. The boys sometimes would ride their scooters around the yard; maybe one boy was rolling an old bicycle frame wheel with a stick, padding it around the yard. We made our own games, and we were so happy when our parents would tell us to go outside and play.

We were contented children, and we loved the outdoors and enjoyed the rainy season because we did not have to bring water from the main government pipe to fill our drums and buckets. The rain was a good deed for us, and we appreciated it. The neighbors were very caring and supportive of one another, looking after their children and other people's children. There is an old saying, "It takes a village to raise a child," and that is true. If anything happened when a parent was not home, they reported the problems and would also do the right thing.

History of the Trinidad Festival

The people portrayed many types of costumes from the different continents of Africa, and this festival came from the slavery days. The slave masters had given the people one day a year to dress up in their traditional attires from where they originated, whether Africa and India. As time went by, it became an elaborate festival, and people made all types of costumes for that special day named the Trinidad Carnival. Now it has become a bigger event, as people have migrate to different parts of the world, such as America, Canada, United Kingdom, and the rest of the Caribbean islands; now they celebrate it with massive costumes. In Trinidad, it is known as Trinidad Carnival; in Canada, it is known as Caribana; and in America, it is known as Labor Day West Indian Parade Celebration.

It is one of the biggest celebrations in the country, and millions of people from all over the world take part in this event. This is the time when people dress in extravagant, beautiful costumes, music is played in the streets, and people of all nationalities danced in the streets.

When I was a child, there were live brass music and the steel bands on the streets accompanied with huge parades of masqueraders on the road and extremely lovely costumes; some wore frightening attires that I and other children were terrified of. I was petrified of a masquerader named Jab Jab, who had a horrible mask face and cracked willows and whips. I was afraid. I would hide myself behind an adult or under a table, and my younger siblings and other children were also scared.

For the carnival festival, the children made their own costumes and face masks to celebrate the carnival's event.My brother and his friends made their own face masks and fashioned their outfits by cutting holes and dyeing their clothing.

They went around the neighborhood to display their attire and received money for their masquerader's outfits. They made their face masks mold by forming it with cow dung and dirt. Then it was mixed together and formed into an ugly face mask, using flour paste and applying several pieces of newspapers. It was placed on a piece of thinning and left to dry in the sun. When the face mask was fully dried, it was carved out and painted, a piece of elastic was applied, and it was ready for use. Whatever we needed, we created for ourselves; those were the days when parents did not have the finances to purchase toys or costumes.

 I will always cherish those wonderful days and never forget the happiest time of my childhood and the memory of the frogs sitting on the lily pads in the pond at the backyard. Everything was so green, so peaceful, and most of all, filled with fresh air. I will always remember the cocks crowing early in the morning. We acknowledged the sounds of the cock crowing as though they were saying, "Co-coo-doo, my father lost his gold shoes," not forgetting the green meadows with various flowers growing wild and the cows grazing on the pasture.

We had lots of fun and played quite a bit in our yard or in the meadow. I loved to see the frogs sitting on lily pads in the pond, and everything was so green and freshly scented. Now I am older, and I think about the golden days; sometimes, I wish I can get a glance of the years that passed by. The streets were lavished with all kinds of fruits, red hibiscus hanging on the fences, and colorful butterflies that flew or sat on the marigolds, the daffodils, or the roses.

History of My Generation

I was informed by an old man who knew my mother's father, who told me that my grandfather came from the Ibo tribe, and he was a merchant; and lived on the border of Morocco. He was a handsome tall fair-skinned man, and he travelled back and forth to Africa. He liked real estate and had bought many acres of land in Trinidad. Because of his complexion, he was never a slave; he was an overseer over the slaves that worked in the sugarcane plantations. People called him Sir Johnny Edwards; he rode a horse and had a watch on a gold chain, which hung at the side of his pants. He was very kind to the people and kept a nation dance once a year for the folks, and they all adored him. He died in 1946.

Dreams do Come True

I did not become a teacher or a professor but became a nurse, fashion designer, author, and artist. As a charge nurse, I still had the teaching privileges to assist the health-care aids about certain nursing procedures. Now I am volunteering my time to students who are interested in becoming a fashion designer and sharing my knowledge about modeling and the fashion business. At least I had followed my dreams as a child to be a writer, artist, and teacher. As a seven-year-old girl, I had written and drawn on every house post and could read any book. Moreover, sometimes dreams do come true. Even though it took many years to accomplish, I still made it. I thank God that I appreciate the good, the bad, and the ugly days of my childhood. One thing I know is to try again and try again until you succeed at last. Hopefully, children will be taught to make their own toys, and it will give them a sense of awareness and creativeness that they are contributing to sustain the environment. Sometimes, it is good for youths to go outside in the yard and play some kind of game, and this can help them to be more alert of their surroundings and Mother Nature. They will be much healthier and energetic. It is also a good exercise for them, instead of staying indoors and watching television or playing video games constantly. Making their own toys and games will make them proud of their originality and ability. Moreover, they will experience how to save money by creating their own projects. It will give them confidence and motivation and inspire them to go after bigger ventures. Most of all, it will boost their self-assurance and vision that nothing can stop them from achieving their goal when they are older and wiser.

I must say that I enjoyed those years even though our parents were very strict. When they said to us "Jump!" we said "How high?"
Written by **Marie Bethel**

About the Author

MARIE BETHEL
SENIOR FASHION DESIGNER, AUTHOR, ARTIST, AND SCULPTOR

Marie Bethel was born in Trinidad and educated in Trinidad, Canada, USA, and United Kingdom. She has obtained a business accountant diploma while attending Alberta Vocational College, studied nursing, and had a successful career. She had a natural love for fashion designing, tailoring her own line of nursing uniforms for colleagues and friends. This passion grew to a need she had to explore.

In 1982 Marie acted on her passion, attending various designing courses and fashion schools, and was finally accepted as a student at the International Academy of Designs and Merchandising in Toronto, Canada. In 1996 the self-motivated young designer graduated, receiving a diploma as a certified fashion designer. After graduating, she worked in New York as a freelance designer and designed costumes and evening wear dresses for the annual Labor Day Caribbean Carnival festival.

In 1998 Marie studied at the Manhattanville Needle Trade School in the Bronx, New York, as a tailor while continuing to work as a freelance designer. To further her knowledge in fashion, she relocated to London, England, United Kingdom, to pursue her career as a designer in 2005, attending the University of Arts London, School of Fashion, while designing clothes for local clients, including Mr. Malcolm Stewart, director of Gallia Textiles, United Kingdom.

In 2006 Marie graduated as a pattern technologist, using the Gerber system, Mac, PC, Illustration, and Photoshop. In 2007 she was fortunate to bond a new working relationship with her soon-to-be mentor and employer, Mr. Albert Alinterdonato, working as an assistant designer in the House of Albert in Florida, USA. Adapting and developing quickly, she soon became one of Mr. Albert's head designers in 2009. She headed her own fashion line, Couturier Fashions, as a separate project, modeling couture and evening dresses.

In 2006 Marie graduated as a pattern technologist, using the Gerber system, Mac, PC, Illustration, and Photoshop. In 2007 she was fortunate to bond a new working relationship with her soon-to-be mentor and employer, Mr. Albert Alinterdonato, working as an assistant designer in the House of Albert in Florida, USA. Adapting and developing quickly, she soon became one of Mr. Albert's head designers in 2009. She headed her own fashion line, Couturier Fashions, as a separate project, modeling couture and evening dresses.

She has been in many fashion shows as well as charity events such as Fashion Island and donated a wedding dress and designed an evening gown, using natural fabrics for a famous woman named Alice Austen; her design was auctioned and put into the museum of Alice Austen House in Fashion Island. She then designed Miss Penny for breast cancer awareness in 2014. The Miss Penny gown was designed with over five thousand pennies and fifty-five dollars in nickels and dimes, using Canadian and American coins. This was posted in CURVY magazine, with the Miss Penny slogan: "Every Penny Counts."

She created Miss Bread for breast cancer awareness from old bread, bread skins, and other household ingredients to honor all the women who lost loved ones and experienced this awful disease called breast cancer. The design has its unique look, with the silhouette and proportions designed as architectural impressions. This bread sculptor turned out to be a beautiful high-fashion model. Her gown has three thousand and two hundred rhinestones with pink ribbons and furs; her necklace was also formed with several rhinestones. It is an extremely elegant piece of artwork. Miss Bread and Miss Penny are registered publications of artwork in Canada. She named this project Miss Bread with the slogan "Thou shalt not live by bread alone, but also donate to breast cancer." The numerous nipple icons on her gown are a reminder of healthy breasts and the unfortunate women that lost the battle and died from breast cancer.

She is also a contributor to two books, The Power of My Faith from Athens Publishing and also Recycling and Renewable Energy from Lovely Silks Publishing. Marie made another contribution to a recipe book entitled Recipes That Make You Go Mmm from Lovely Silks Publishing. She invented banana bread chocolate muffin and honey chocolate. Now she has written a children's book entitled Back in Time and did all the illustrations. It will be on the market soon through Authors Tranquility Press publishing company.

The numerous nipple icons on her gown are a reminder of healthy breasts and the unfortunate women that lost the battle and died from breast cancer.

She is also a contributor to two books, The Power of My Faith from Athens Publishing and also Recycling and Renewable Energy from Lovely Silks Publishing. Marie made another contribution to a recipe book entitled Recipes That Make You Go Mmm from Lovely Silks Publishing. She invented banana bread chocolate muffin and honey chocolate. Now she has written a children's book entitled Back in Time and did all the illustrations. It will be on the market soon through Authors Tranquility Press publishing company.

Marie started a new project called M3A Designs, which recycles clothing by recreating the old to the new, using bridal gowns, eveningwear, men's suits, jeans, and any type of clothing that can redesigned into a fabulous, fashionable, young, fresh look. She combined her respect for timeless design with a sensibility for flattering silhouettes and started affordable recycled-clothing needs without compromising her eco-sensitive lifestyle. As this business grew, seamstresses have been recruited from women's shelters. They have the satisfaction of working on one garment from start to finish and offering creative input.

The fashion world is buzzing and looking for new, fresh ideas to elevate the industry, and the time has come from the very creative Marie Bethel to shake things up. She believes in creating a one-of-a-kind garment. Her patience, hard work, and years of experience have paid off indeed.

Visit her website: http://www.m3ahouseoffashion.com/.

www.ingramcontent.com/pod-product-compliance
Lightning Source LLC
LaVergne TN
LVHW070222080526
838202LV00068B/6884